Together

Written and Compiled by Miriam Hathaway | Designed by Heidi Dyer

Together

We make a difference.

There's a lot to say about the connection we share. And there's a lot to celebrate about the ways we lean on, lift up, stretch, and strengthen each other. We might be friends, family, partners, or companions. No matter what we are to each other, we have built a community. The effects we have on each other ripple out in a thousand ways, to people beyond us and to places we haven't even been.

—— *This is the quiet magic of our togetherness.*
We can be more than ourselves, together.

Together

Our true selves shine brightly, spontaneously.

A GOOD FRIEND IS A CONNECTION TO LIFE...

———— *Lois Wyse*

Together

We bring joy to whatever we do, wherever we go, and whomever we're with.

HAPPINESS IS NOT PERFECTED UNTIL IT IS SHARED.

—————— *Jane Porter*

Together

We become something bigger.

THROUGH LOVE, THROUGH FRIENDSHIP,

A HEART LIVES MORE THAN ONE LIFE...

———— *Anaïs Nin*

Together

Our support is steadfast and true.

A FRIEND IS WHAT THE HEART NEEDS ALL THE TIME.

———— *Henry van Dyke*

Together

We stand up for what we believe in.

LIFE WOULD BE DULL INDEED WITHOUT EXPERIMENTERS AND COURAGEOUS BREAKERS-WITH-TRADITION.

———— *Marie Bullock*

There are those whose lives affect all others around them... Reaching out to ends further than they would ever know.

———— *William Bradfield*

Together

*We see things clearly and are honest
with each other and ourselves.*

REMEMBER THAT WHEREVER YOUR HEART IS,
THERE YOU WILL FIND YOUR TREASURE.

———— *Paulo Coelho*

Together

*We know when to play, when to laugh,
and when to lighten things up.*

THOSE WHO BRING SUNSHINE TO THE LIVES
OF OTHERS CANNOT KEEP IT FROM THEMSELVES.

——— *J. M. Barrie*

Together

We share warmth and affection.

WHEN YOU'RE WITH A FRIEND,

YOUR HEART HAS COME HOME.

——— *Emily Farrar*

Together

---

*We know it's okay to make mistakes
and learn from them.*

A LOVING HEART IS THE TRUEST WISDOM.

———— *Charles Dickens*

Together

We know generosity wins.

WE MUST NOT ONLY GIVE WHAT WE HAVE,

WE MUST ALSO GIVE WHAT WE ARE.

——— *Désiré-Joseph Mercier*

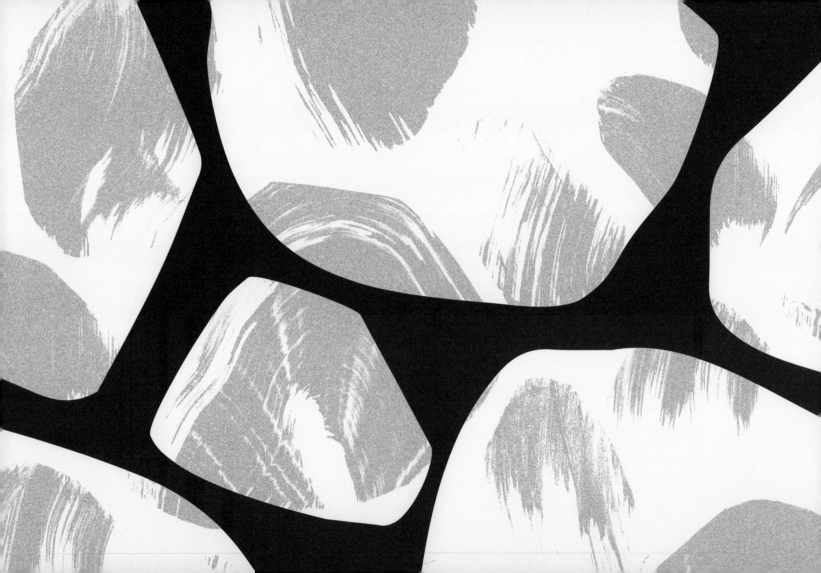

...the capacity to care is the thing which gives life its deepest significance.

———— *Pablo Casals*

Together

We hold each other in the painful moments.

WITHIN US IS GREAT STRENGTH,

AN ABILITY TO OVERCOME AND TO ENDURE.

———— *Nicole Braddock*

Together

We see possibility, even in the wildest circumstances.

THERE IS NOTHING WE CANNOT LIVE DOWN,
AND RISE ABOVE, AND OVERCOME.

———— *Ella Wheeler Wilcox*

Together

We are always ready for adventure.

NO ROAD IS LONG WITH GOOD COMPANY.

——— *Turkish Proverb*

Together

We honor each other's spoken and unspoken wishes.

WE SPEAK WITH MORE THAN OUR MOUTHS.

WE LISTEN WITH MORE THAN OUR EARS.

———— *Fred Rogers*

Together

We can all change and grow.

OPEN HEARTS WILL OPEN MORE HEARTS.

——— *Cat Forsley*

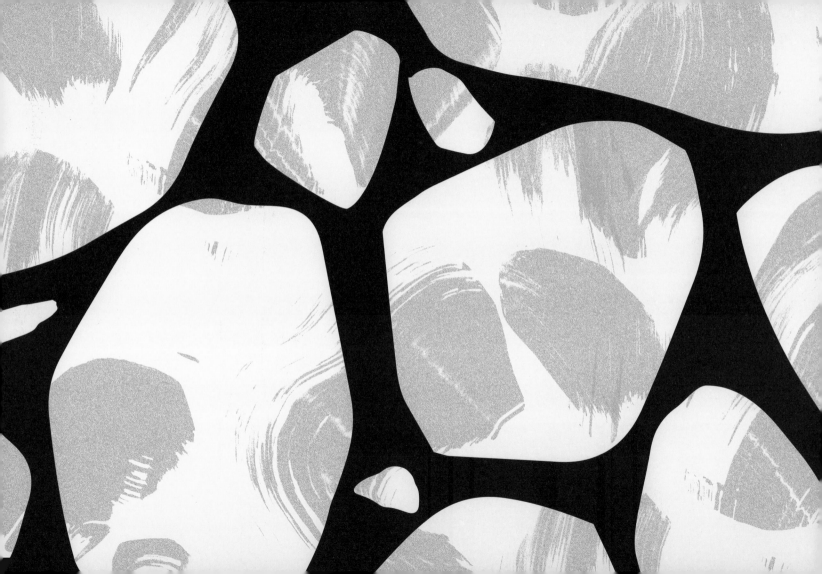

Where you are understood, you are at home.

——— *John O'Donohue*

Together

We pull away from each other and come
back to each other with grace.

TIME DOESN'T TAKE AWAY FROM TRUE
FRIENDSHIP, NOR DOES SEPARATION.

———— *Tennessee Williams*

Together

We are confident, allowing others to be confident too.

IT TAKES EACH OF US TO MAKE
A DIFFERENCE FOR ALL OF US.

———— *Jackie Mutcheson*

Together

We feel safe showing our feelings.

WHEN SOMEONE TELLS YOU THE TRUTH,
LETS YOU THINK FOR YOURSELF, EXPERIENCE
YOUR OWN EMOTIONS, HE IS TREATING YOU
AS A TRUE EQUAL. AS A FRIEND.

———— *Whitney Otto*

Together

*We can easily depend on each other, knowing
when we need to linger a little longer.*

STAY IS A CHARMING WORD IN A FRIEND'S VOCABULARY.

——— *Amos Bronson Alcott*

Together

We build unwavering trust.

GOOD FRIENDS ARE LIKE STARS. YOU DON'T ALWAYS SEE THEM,
BUT YOU KNOW THEY ARE ALWAYS THERE.

———— *Unknown*

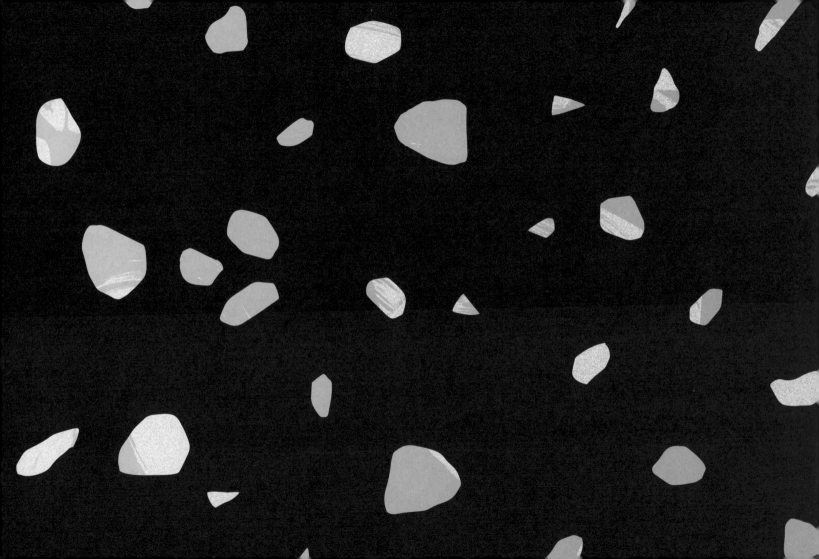

The work of your heart, the work of
taking time, to listen, to help, is also
your gift to the whole of the world.

——— *Jack Kornfield*

Together

We encourage each other to become our best selves.

...AS WE LET OUR OWN LIGHT SHINE, WE UNCONSCIOUSLY

GIVE OTHER PEOPLE PERMISSION TO DO THE SAME.

———— *Marianne Williamson*

Together

We're inspired by everything that makes us who we are.

THE LANGUAGE OF FRIENDSHIP IS NOT WORDS BUT MEANINGS.

——————— *Henry David Thoreau*

Together

We share uplifting smiles.

YOUR SPARK CAN BECOME A FLAME
AND CHANGE EVERYTHING.

———— *E. D. Nixon*

Together

*We open our hearts, expand our world,
and spread kindness.*

CELEBRATE THAT WHICH YOU SHARE WITH OTHERS.
FOR THEIR JOY, HAPPINESS, AND LOVE SHALL BRING
YOU WEALTH BEYOND MEASURE.

————— *Rio Godfrey*

Together

We change things for the better.

WITH LOVE AND PATIENCE, NOTHING IS IMPOSSIBLE.

——— *Daisaku Ikeda*

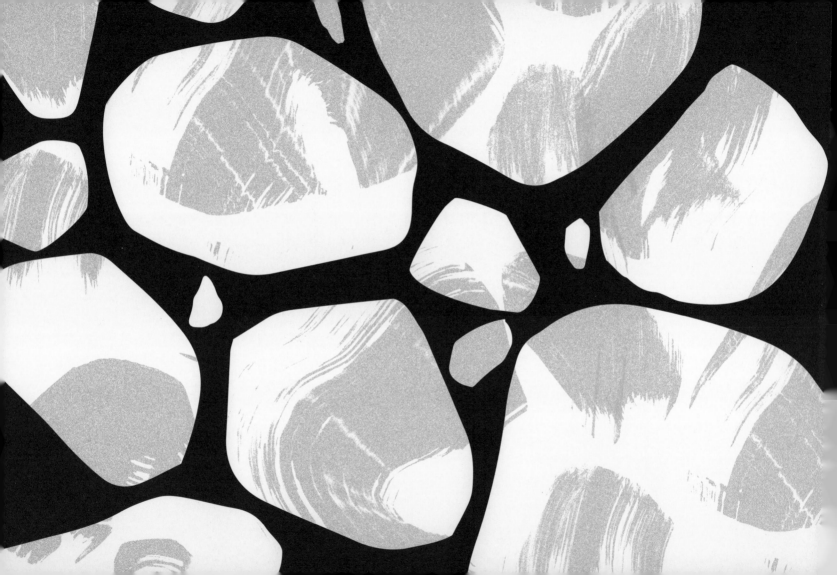

We'll do it together.

———— *Molly Fumia*

COMPENDIUM.
live inspired

Written and Compiled by: Miriam Hathaway
Designed by: Heidi Dyer | Edited by: Ruth Austin

LIBRARY OF CONGRESS CONTROL NUMBER: 2019949587 / ISBN: 978-1-970147-00-1

1st printing. Printed in China with soy and metallic inks on FSC®–Mix certified paper.

Create meaningful moments with gifts that inspire.

CONNECT WITH US
live-inspired.com | sayhello@compendiuminc.com

@compendiumliveinspired
#compendiumliveinspired